Weaving Hearts:

Battling Loneliness

Embracing Belonging

A self-help guide to combat loneliness.

Krist Pereira

Index

Part 6: Practicing Self-care and nourishment
Mindfulness, meditation, and relaxation techniques
Guided mindfulness exercise: Practicing self-acceptance and relaxation
Engaging in activities that bring joy and fulfillment

Part 7: Keeping Personal Relationships Alive
Re-ignite Long-Term Personal Connections
Sustaining meaningful relationships over time
Dealing with conflicts and challenges in relationships

Part 8: Nurturing Social Connections
Importance of building and maintaining supportive relationships
Communication skills for deepening connections
Promoting empathy, compassion, and understanding in interpersonal relationships

Part 9: Embracing Technology Mindfully
Using technology as a tool for connection rather than a barrier
Balancing online interactions with face-to-face communication
Setting boundaries and managing screen time to prioritize real-life connections

Part 10: Embracing Community and Support
The importance of participating in inclusive and supportive environments
Embrace a sense of belonging in local communities, workplaces, and online spaces
Create your support network

Part 11: Taking Action and Moving Forward
Creating a personalized action plan for combating loneliness
Setting realistic goals and tracking progress
Celebrating successes and staying motivated on the journey
towards building meaningful connections

Part 12: Seeking Professional Support
When to consider therapy or counseling for loneliness
Different therapeutic approaches for addressing loneliness
and related mental health issues
Resources for finding affordable or free mental health
support

Conclusion: Thriving Together
Reflecting on the journey of overcoming loneliness and
building a fulfilling life
Encouragement to continue prioritizing social connections
and self-acceptance and care
Inspiring stories of individuals who have successfully
overcome loneliness and found happiness

A loneliness prayer

In the heart's quiet chamber, where shadows dwell,

Loneliness whispers its sorrowful tale.

But amidst the darkness, a light shines bright,

A beacon of hope in the stillness of night.

Through trials and triumphs, we journey on,

Seeking solace in the bonds we've drawn.

With each step forward, we find our way,

Towards a future bathed in the light of day.

So let us stand together, hand in hand,

United in purpose, a resilient band.

For in our connection, we find our worth,

And in our shared joy, we find our rebirth.

As the echoes of loneliness fade away,

We embrace the promise of a brighter day.

For in thriving together, we truly see,

The beauty of life's interconnected decree.

- Krist Pereira, 2024

"Loneliness and the feeling of being unwanted is the most terrible poverty."

 - Mother Teresa

Introduction

Hi, I am Krist, your new companion at this point. I am excited to share this time with you. There could be multiple reasons why you have turned to this book, but I can assure you that if you follow and practice what lies within this book you will seldom be lonely or let another human being be left lonely. You are going to be the change in your own life. So let's begin!

You hold the power to rewrite the story of your life, to banish loneliness from your doorstep, and to radiate warmth and compassion to all who cross your path.

Loneliness is a silent epidemic that permeates our society, affecting millions of lives in profound and often unseen ways. It's a pervasive ache, an emptiness that gnaws at the soul, leaving us feeling disconnected, isolated, and adrift in a sea of faces or places. But amidst the shadows of loneliness, there lies a glimmer of hope – the transformative power of connection.

So what is the most common emotion you experience? Is it being lonely? Is it feeling being alone, even when amidst others? Do you choose to hide away from the world because of your personal insecurities and the perceptions in your mind? Or is it that you really enjoy solitude, where you actually find inner power?

In this book, we embark on a journey to unravel the complexities of loneliness, shine a light on its root causes, and discover practical approaches for forging meaningful connections and reclaiming our sense of belonging. We confront the staggering magnitude of the problem, acknowledging its grave impact on mental, emotional, and physical well-being. Yet, we also embrace the boundless potential for healing, growth, and resilience within each of us.

By delving into the pages of this book, you will embark on a transformative journey of self-discovery and empowerment. You will gain insight into the subtle nuances of loneliness, uncovering the underlying factors that contribute to its grip on our lives. You will explore practical tools for breaking free from the cycle of loneliness, nurturing supportive relationships, and cultivating a deeper sense of purpose, connection and fulfillment.

I highly recommend you have a diary or journal with you to write your thoughts and understanding as you go through the exercise. Later you can use this to reflect on what you have learnt and visualize your amazing journey.

The intent of this book is not to make you a master on the subject of loneliness, being alone or finding peace in solitude. The sole purpose is to give you the confidence and assurance that you don't need to fight your battles on your own. Gain courage and strength to commit to a better life. One of purpose, meaning and gratitude.

Purchasing this book isn't just an investment in personal growth – it's a declaration of resilience, a commitment to reclaiming your joy and vitality. It serves as a beacon of hope for anyone who has ever felt the sting of loneliness, offering practical guidance and support to navigate the challenges and uncertainties of life.

Each day countless people choose to end their lives because they feel lonely and hopeless. And not because they are poor or facing financial difficulties or victims of abuse. In my years of working with numerous individuals, it doesn't matter what your circumstances are, it's just your willingness to be fully committed to change that truly makes the difference. You can do it!

Consider sharing or gifting this book to someone you know who may be experiencing loneliness – a friend, a family member, a colleague – and offer them the gift of connection, understanding, and hope.

Together, let us unlock the power of our mind, embracing the journey toward healing, growth, and fulfillment. For in our shared humanity, we find strength, resilience, and the promise of a brighter tomorrow.

I thank you for taking the time to reflect on the contents within this book and do hope you reach out to at least one person to make a difference.

Thank you,

Krist Pereira

Author, Keynote Speaker and Mindset coach

"The greatest loneliness is to not be comfortable with yourself."

- Mark Twain

Part 1: Getting to know loneliness

Loneliness is something we all experience at some point in our lives, regardless of who we are. It's not just about being alone; it's about feeling disconnected from others, even when we're surrounded by people. This feeling of emptiness or longing for companionship can affect our mental and physical health in profound ways.

In today's world, where we're more connected than ever through technology, it might seem strange that so many people feel lonely. But factors like social isolation, changes in family life, and the fast pace of modern life can all contribute to this sense of loneliness.

It's important to understand that loneliness is different from solitude. While loneliness feels sad and isolating, solitude is when we choose to spend time alone for reflection or relaxation. Solitude can actually be a good thing—it gives us a chance to recharge and discover ourselves.

But chronic loneliness, the kind that sticks around for a long time, can be really harmful. It's been linked to mental health issues like depression and anxiety, as well as physical problems like heart disease and a weakened immune system. So it's crucial to address feelings of loneliness and find ways to reconnect with others for our overall well-being.

In 2023, a survey from Nextdoor in partnership with Marmalade Trust, UK revealed that 85% of UK adults had experienced loneliness in the last 12 months. Almost half (44%) felt chronically lonely. [1]

---

[1] Source https://www.marmaladetrust.org/loneliness-guide

Definition of Loneliness

Loneliness is a subjective feeling of isolation or lack or complete loss of connection with others, even when surrounded by people. It is characterized by a sense of emptiness, sadness, or longing for social interaction and meaningful relationships.

Prevalence and Impact of Loneliness:

Loneliness is a widespread phenomenon that affects individuals of all ages and backgrounds. Research has shown that chronic loneliness can have profound effects on both mental and physical health. It has been linked to an increased risk of depression, anxiety, substance abuse, cardiovascular disease, and even premature death. Additionally, loneliness can impair cognitive function, weaken the immune system, and lead to poor sleep quality.

Loneliness can affect anyone. Experiences of loneliness can vary, but its effects can be profound and wide-ranging. It is considered by many to be one of the largest public health challenges we face.

- In 2022, 49.63% of adults (25.99 million people) in the UK reported feeling lonely occasionally, sometimes, often or always
- Approximately 7.1% of people in Great Britain (3.83 million) experience chronic loneliness, meaning they feel lonely 'often or always'.

- This has risen from 6% (3.24 million) in 2020, indicating that there has not been a return to pre-pandemic levels of loneliness .

- The latest facts and statistics about loneliness help us to understand more about the **risk factors** and the impact it can have on different areas of our lives.

By increasing the evidence base, we can help to inform policy and practice to address loneliness. [2]

Nearly one in four people worldwide -- which translates into more than a billion people -- feel very or fairly lonely, according to a recent Meta-Gallup survey of more than 140 countries.[3]

On May 2, the U.S. surgeon general, Dr. Vivek Murthy, sounded the alarm about an American epidemic which predated COVID-19: the phenomenon of reported loneliness, now affecting half of all Americans. It is a serious problem. Lack of social connection, according to one dramatic formulation, has been found to be as dangerous as smoking up to 15 cigarettes a day.[4]

---

[2] https://www.campaigntoendloneliness.org/facts-and-statistics/

[3] https://news.gallup.com/opinion/gallup/512618/almost-quarter-world-feels-lonely.aspx?thank-you-subscription-form=1

[4] https://www.capita.org/capita-ideas/2023/05/16/what-the-surgeon-general-missed-about-americas-loneliness-epidemic1?gad_source=1&gclid=Cj0KCQjw2a6wBhCVARIsABPeH1uk88JOlHj-jjoY0bVFoa4iSwF1WGo3bCBrfRoh9ITZ2OP1ak5aHfkaAm-zEALw_wcB

Exercise 1 :

Here is a short quiz that will aid your understanding of loneliness and challenge common misconceptions about this complex emotion. Take your time to consider each statement before selecting your answer.

Please mark each statement as True or False.

1. Loneliness only affects older adults.

2. Loneliness is the same as being alone.

3. Social media can effectively alleviate feelings of loneliness.

4. Loneliness has no significant impact on physical health.

5. Loneliness is a temporary emotion that everyone experiences from time to time.

6. Loneliness is solely determined by the number of social connections a person has.

7. Loneliness is more prevalent in urban areas compared to rural areas.

8. Loneliness is a common experience among adolescents and young adults.

9. Loneliness can be alleviated simply by being in the presence of others.

10. Chronic loneliness is often caused by external factors beyond an individual's control.

11. Loneliness is more common among introverts than extroverts.

12. Loneliness and social isolation are interchangeable terms.

13. Loneliness is associated with an increased risk of developing certain chronic diseases.

14. Loneliness can be passed down through generations within families.

15. Engaging in social activities automatically guarantees protection against loneliness.

16. Loneliness is primarily a psychological issue and does not impact physical health.

17. People who experience loneliness are more likely to engage in risky behaviors.

18. Building deep and meaningful connections with others can help alleviate loneliness.

19. Loneliness is more prevalent among single individuals compared to those in relationships.

20. Seeking professional help is not necessary for overcoming loneliness.

Answer key:

1. False 2. False 3. False 4. False 5. True 6. False 7. True

8. True 9. False 10. True 11. False 12. False 13. True 14. False

15. False 16. False 17. True 18. True 19. False 20. False

Exercise 2 :

Reflecting on Personal Experiences of Loneliness

Take a few moments to reflect on your own experiences of loneliness. Consider times when you have felt disconnected from others or experienced a sense of isolation.

- How often do you feel a sense of isolation or being lonely?
- What were the circumstances surrounding these feelings?
- What made you feel the need to be silent or isolated?
- How did it impact your mood, behavior, and overall well-being?
- What did you do to move out of this experience?

Reflecting on these experiences can help deepen your understanding of loneliness and its effects on your life or the others around you. Remember you don't have to rush through the book but rather complete each exercise as you go along to achieve the best results.

Part 2: What Makes Us Feel Lonely

Exploring the depths of loneliness requires understanding its underlying causes, which are as diverse as the individuals experiencing them. Within this chapter, we embark on a journey to uncover these roots, illuminating the myriad factors that sow seeds of isolation in our lives.

By shedding light on these hidden triggers, we pave the way for crafting a personalized approach to confront and overcome loneliness head-on.

While every attempt has been made to highlight most prominent causes, there will be others that may need to be highlighted but not covered here. However, the key here is to identify what is most closely related to the cause of your pain.

Social or Cultural Isolation:
One of the primary contributors to loneliness is social isolation. This can occur when individuals lack meaningful connections with others due to geographical distance, physical barriers, or a lack of social or cultural support networks.

Gender Identity:
For those whose gender identity aligns with societal expectations, navigating relationships and social spaces may be comparatively

smoother. However, for transgender, non-binary, and gender non-conforming individuals, the journey can be fraught with challenges. Discrimination, stigma, and rejection from family, friends, and society at large can lead to feelings of isolation and alienation. Moreover, the struggle to authentically express one's gender identity in a world that often invalidates or erases it can contribute to a deep sense of loneliness. This pervasive loneliness can stem from a lack of understanding and acceptance, making it crucial for society to foster inclusivity, respect, and affirmation for individuals of all gender identities, thus combating the roots of loneliness at their core.

Rani, a 25-year-old transgender woman, experienced acute loneliness primarily due to societal norms and familial rejection stemming from her gender identity. Growing up in a conservative community where discussions about gender diversity were scarce, Rani faced significant pushback from her family and peers when she openly explored her true identity. This lack of acceptance and understanding in her immediate environment contributed to feelings of isolation and abandonment, exacerbating her sense of loneliness.

Societal Norms:
Societal norms and expectations surrounding relationships, marriage, and family can also play a significant role in shaping

feelings of loneliness. Individuals who do not conform to these norms may experience social exclusion and feelings of inadequacy.

Sarah, a single woman in her thirties, often feels pressure from society to settle down and start a family. Despite her fulfilling career and active social life, Sarah can't help but feel a sense of loneliness and isolation at times, as she grapples with societal expectations and her own desires for companionship.

Life Transitions:

Change is constant! Events are just part of life, good, bad or ugly! Whether by choice or circumstance, such as moving to a new city, starting a new job, or experiencing a significant loss, which can disrupt social connections and exacerbate feelings of loneliness. These transitions often involve periods of adjustment and uncertainty, during which individuals may feel isolated and disconnected from others.

Anna, a recent college graduate, moved to a new city for a job opportunity. Despite her excitement for this new chapter in her life, she found herself feeling lonely and isolated in her new surroundings. Without the familiar support network of friends and family, Anna struggled to establish meaningful connections and navigate her newfound independence.

Professional and career choices

The weight of professional responsibility and the relentless pressure to meet expectations can often lead to feelings of loneliness in individuals. As individuals pour their time and energy into their careers, they may find themselves sacrificing meaningful connections and neglecting their social and emotional well-being. The demanding nature of certain professions, coupled with long hours and high levels of stress, can create a sense of isolation as individuals struggle to balance work and personal life. Moreover, the competitive nature of many workplaces may foster a culture where vulnerability and seeking support are perceived as signs of weakness, further exacerbating feelings of loneliness. Over time, the relentless pursuit of professional success can leave individuals feeling disconnected from their colleagues, friends, and even themselves, ultimately contributing to a deep sense of loneliness.

Stacey, a successful marketing executive, dedicated her life to climbing the corporate ladder. Yet, beneath her achievements, she grappled with intense loneliness. Long hours and high-pressure demands left her feeling isolated and overwhelmed. As the weight of her responsibilities grew heavier, Stacey's mental health deteriorated. Suicidal thoughts became a constant presence in her darkest moments.

Sudden loss of relationship or loved ones:

The abrupt departure of a significant relationship or the unexpected death of a loved one can shatter one's sense of stability and security, leaving behind a profound emptiness and overwhelming grief that can intensify feelings of loneliness and isolation.

Kate felt profound loneliness after her husband, James, passed away suddenly. Despite support from loved ones, she grappled with emptiness and isolation, longing for James's comforting presence. Tasks became overwhelming, and she withdrew from social interactions, feeling disconnected from others.

Mental Health Issues:

Mental health conditions such as depression, anxiety, and low self-esteem can contribute to feelings of loneliness. Individuals struggling with these issues may find it challenging to engage with others, leading to social withdrawal and isolation.

Mark has battled depression for several years, and his condition has often left him feeling isolated and disconnected from those around him. Despite having a supportive family and friends, Mark struggles to reach out and connect with others, fearing judgment and rejection.

Self-doubts/negative thoughts: This internal dialogue can breed feelings of unworthiness and apprehension about forming connections, often stemming from a fear of rejection and a sense of inadequacy.

After attending a social gathering, Jane couldn't shake the feeling that she didn't belong. She replayed conversations in her mind, convinced that she had said something wrong or made a fool of herself. This internal dialogue left her feeling unworthy of forming connections and apprehensive about future interactions, feeding into her fear of rejection and reinforcing a sense of inadequacy.

Past or Present trauma/negative experiences: Lingering scars from past or present traumas or negative experiences can create barriers to forming new connections, as individuals may struggle with trust issues, fear of vulnerability, and emotional wounds that affect their ability to engage with others.

After experiencing betrayal in a previous relationship, Rob found it difficult to trust others. The emotional wounds from his past trauma made him hesitant to open up or form new connections. Fear of vulnerability kept him guarded, preventing him from fully engaging with others and hindering his ability to build meaningful relationships.

Vulnerability: The courage to open oneself up to others, risking rejection and hurt in the pursuit of genuine connection, yet also offering the opportunity for deep empathy, understanding, and authentic relationships to flourish.

After losing his job unexpectedly, Pete struggled with feelings of insecurity and inadequacy. The experience left him emotionally scarred, making it challenging for him to trust others in professional settings. Fear of vulnerability kept him guarded, hindering his ability to network effectively and advance in his career. Despite his talents and qualifications, Pete's reluctance to open up and connect with others held him back from achieving his full potential.

Social media: While offering a platform for connection, it can also amplify feelings of inadequacy and fear of rejection, as individuals compare themselves to curated images of others' lives, fostering self-doubt and negative thoughts.

Tom's heart raced as he reluctantly unlocked his phone, with trembling fingers, he scrolled through the feed. Each image and update served as a painful reminder of what he had lost. Seeing his ex-partner's smiling face among mutual friends' posts was like a knife to his already wounded heart, reopening old wounds and fueling feelings of betrayal and abandonment. The fear of rejection and inadequacy consumed him as he compared his fractured reality to the seemingly perfect lives of others, amplifying his sense of isolation and despair.

There will be many more such instances where you could find yourself in a mindspace of loneliness. It can be a good place to be in and self reflect on the true meaning of life and existence. I've known many individuals who have used this experience to actually transform their lives into very meaningful pursuits. Building a new bucket list, setting new goals or taking up challenges activities etc. In contrast, for many or most this can be truly challenging in a very negative way. Slipping into a downward spiral of helplessness, defeat and sadness. It is in these moments when our minds begin to trick us into hopelessness, fear and doubt that we leave ourselves most vulnerable.

The reality we think we perceive is limited to our thoughts, feelings and emotions. Often completely disconnected from the world of possibility that lies right within us and around us. A world that we can create and thrive in. If only we learn to train the voice in mind to visualize, believe and accept what we truly want. And yes it is possible. Only if you believe it in your mind.

If you're truly dedicated to overcoming loneliness in your life, I urge you to invest the time in answering the following questions with as much depth as possible.

Folks, this is incredibly important and serves as one of the primary motivations behind writing this book. Gaining an awareness of the cause or trigger is very important.

We cannot change the past but we have the power to create new thoughts of the present by gaining understanding and knowledge. Create new positive images in our mind of what we want our future to be like. With the right mindset, we can create what we truly desire. This is so important and true.

Exercise 3:

These questions will prompt you to reflect on your own experiences of loneliness, identify potential triggers and coping mechanisms, and explore ways for breaking the cycle of loneliness.

1. Can you identify specific situations or circumstances that tend to trigger feelings of loneliness for you?

2. How does social media usage impact your feelings of loneliness?

3. Have you experienced any major life transitions recently (e.g., moving to a new city, starting a new job) that have contributed to feelings of loneliness?

4. Do you find it challenging to initiate or maintain social connections due to factors such as shyness or social anxiety?

5. Have you experienced any significant changes in your social support network (e.g., loss of friendships, changes in family dynamics) that have impacted your feelings of loneliness?

6. How do you typically cope with feelings of loneliness? Are these coping mechanisms effective in alleviating loneliness in the long term?

7. Are there any negative thought patterns or beliefs that contribute to your feelings of loneliness? If so, what are they?

8. Do you feel comfortable reaching out to others for support when you're feeling lonely? If not, what barriers do you face in seeking help?

9. Have you noticed any patterns in your behavior or lifestyle that may contribute to feelings of loneliness (e.g., spending excessive time alone, avoiding social situations)?

10. Are there any hobbies or interests that bring you joy and fulfillment? How can you incorporate these activities into your life to combat loneliness?

11. Have you ever experienced feelings of loneliness even when surrounded by people? What do you think contributes to this experience?

12. Are there any past traumas or negative experiences that may be influencing your feelings of loneliness? How can you address these underlying issues?

13. Do you have a strong sense of purpose or meaning in your life? How does this impact your feelings of loneliness?

14. Are there any cultural or societal factors that contribute to your experiences of loneliness?

15. Do you feel comfortable expressing your emotions and vulnerabilities to others? How does this impact your ability to connect with people?

16. Have you ever considered seeking professional help or therapy to address feelings of loneliness? What factors have influenced your decision?

17. Are there any changes you can make to your daily routine or environment to reduce feelings of loneliness (e.g., joining social clubs, volunteering)?

18. Do you have a support system in place (e.g., friends, family, support groups) that you can turn to for help when you're feeling lonely?

19. How do you define a meaningful connection with others? What qualities do you value in your relationships?

20. Are there any barriers preventing you from taking action to combat loneliness? How can you overcome these obstacles and implement positive changes in your life?

Understandably, these questions aren't easy to answer by any means, and I don't expect you to tackle them all in one sitting. The key here is to be open and willing to reflect on these challenging questions. This book is designed to serve as a starting point for this journey.

Throughout the following chapters, you'll find additional resources, tools, exercises, and references to support you every step of the way in this process.

- "Connection is the energy that exists between people when they feel seen, heard, and valued." - Brené Brown

Part 3: Breaking the Cycle of Loneliness

Breaking free from the cycle of loneliness requires awareness, self-reflection, and proactive steps toward positive change. In this chapter, we explore how to recognize the signs of loneliness, challenge negative thought patterns, and cultivate self-acceptance and resilience as essential tools for overcoming loneliness.

Being Alone, Lonely, or in Solitude

Being Alone:

Being alone refers to a state of physical isolation, where an individual finds themselves without companionship or company. This state can occur by choice or circumstance and may or may not be accompanied by feelings of loneliness. Being alone can provide opportunities for introspection, relaxation, and independence, but it does not inherently imply loneliness.

Lonely:

Loneliness, on the other hand, is an emotional state characterized by a profound sense of isolation, disconnection, and longing for companionship or connection with others. It can occur even in the presence of people or during social interactions if there is a perceived lack of meaningful connection or understanding. Loneliness can stem from various factors, including social isolation, relationship breakdowns, or internal feelings of inadequacy or unworthiness.

In Solitude:

Solitude differs from both being alone and loneliness in that it represents a deliberate choice to seek out and embrace moments of aloneness for personal reflection, rejuvenation, or spiritual growth. Solitude is a state of being at peace with oneself and finding contentment in one's own company. Unlike loneliness, solitude is not necessarily accompanied by negative emotions; instead, it can be a source of empowerment and self-discovery.

While being alone simply denotes physical separation from others, loneliness encompasses the emotional distress that can arise from perceived social isolation. Solitude, on the other hand, represents a positive and intentional engagement with aloneness, offering opportunities for self-reflection, growth, and inner peace. Understanding these distinctions can help you navigate experiences of aloneness more effectively and cultivate a deeper sense of connection and well-being.

Coping with Periods of Solitude Without Feeling Lonely:

Solitude can be a valuable opportunity for self-reflection, growth, and rejuvenation. Here are some ways to cope with periods of solitude without succumbing to loneliness:

Engage in Solo Activities:

Explore hobbies and interests that bring you joy and fulfillment, whether it's reading, writing, painting, or practicing mindfulness and meditation.

Connect Virtually:

Stay connected with friends and loved ones through virtual platforms and social media, even when physical distance separates you. Schedule virtual gatherings, game nights, or movie marathons to maintain social connections.

Think of solitude as a fertile soil for personal growth and introspection. Just as seeds planted in fertile soil have the opportunity to grow and flourish, periods of solitude provide an opportunity for self-discovery and renewal.

Alex, a busy professional, cherishes his alone time as an opportunity for self-care and reflection. He spends his evenings unwinding with a good book, practicing yoga, and journaling about his thoughts and experiences. Despite enjoying his solitude, Alex stays connected with friends and family through regular phone calls and virtual hangouts.

Recognizing Signs of Loneliness:

Before breaking the cycle of loneliness, it's crucial to recognize the signs and symptoms, both in oneself and in others. These may include feelings of emptiness, sadness, social withdrawal, and a lack of meaningful connections with others.

Exercise 4:

Identifying Personal Triggers and Coping Mechanisms:

Based on your responses to exercise 3 we invite you to reflect on your own experiences of loneliness and identify personal triggers and coping mechanisms. Let's explore the situations, thoughts, and emotions that contribute to the feelings of isolation, as well as ways used to cope with loneliness.

1. **Reflect on past experiences of loneliness:** Think about times when you have felt lonely or isolated. What were the circumstances surrounding these experiences? What thoughts or emotions did you experience?

2. **Identify personal triggers:** Consider the factors or situations that tend to trigger feelings of loneliness for you. These may include specific events, environments, or interactions.

3. **Explore coping mechanisms:** Reflect on the strategies you currently use to cope with loneliness. These may include

reaching out to friends or family members, engaging in activities you enjoy, or practicing self-care techniques.

Journaling about your thoughts and emotions can help bring awareness to underlying patterns.

Practical Tips for Breaking the Cycle of Loneliness:
Once you have identified what makes you feel lonely, you can begin to implement practical techniques to break the cycle and foster meaningful connections.

Some practical tips for combating loneliness may include:

Challenge negative thoughts:
Negative thought patterns and beliefs can perpetuate feelings of loneliness and isolation. These may include thoughts such as "I'm not worthy of love or connection," or "Nobody understands me." By challenging these beliefs and replacing them with more positive and realistic perspectives, we can begin to shift our mindset and break free from the cycle of loneliness. Practice self-compassion and positive self-talk.

Exercise 5:

Identify a negative thought or belief that contributes to feelings of loneliness.

Ask yourself: Is this thought based on fact or perception? What evidence do I have to support or challenge this belief?

Now, try reframing the thought into a more positive and empowering affirmation.

Finding Purpose, meaning and being grateful:

Seeking a life of purpose, meaning, and gratitude, as espoused by motivational speaker Bob Proctor, offers us a transformative approach to breaking the cycle of loneliness. Dr. Proctor's teachings encourage us to focus on what truly matters and by aligning actions with personal values, you can cultivate a sense of fulfillment and connection that transcends social isolation.

By intentionally seeking out opportunities to live authentically and contribute to the greater good, you can break free from the grip of loneliness and find fulfillment in meaningful connections and purposeful living.

Engaging in activities that contribute to the well-being of others or pursuing passions that bring joy and fulfillment fosters a sense of purpose and belonging.

Practicing gratitude for the blessings and connections present in one's life, no matter how small, cultivates a mindset of abundance and appreciation, counteracting feelings of loneliness and isolation.

Through Dr Bob Proctor's messaging, you can learn to harness the power of gratitude, acknowledging the abundance present in your life and fostering a sense of appreciation for the connections and blessings you encounter daily. This proactive approach to personal growth empowers you to cultivate a life rich in purpose, meaning, and gratitude, ultimately breaking free from the shackles of loneliness and embracing a future filled with joy, fulfillment, and authentic connection.

Breaking the cycle of loneliness requires a combination of self-awareness, self-compassion, and proactive steps toward positive change. By recognizing the signs of loneliness, challenging negative thought patterns, and fostering resilience, we can begin to cultivate deeper relationships.

"The quality of your life is the quality of your relationships." - Tony Robbins

Part 4: Combating Loneliness

Building a Mindset Focused on Purpose, Resilience and Results

Loneliness often arises from a lack of connection or sense of purpose which is greater than the current circumstance in our lives. By shifting our mindset to focus on purpose and resilience, we can reframe our experiences and find meaning, even in solitude.

One way to build this mindset is by identifying our values and passions. What is it that we truly desire and what is it we want to become? What brings us joy and fulfillment? What do we care deeply about? By aligning our actions with our values, we can create a sense of purpose that transcends our circumstances.

Additionally, cultivating resilience is crucial in overcoming loneliness. Resilience allows us to bounce back from setbacks and challenges, empowering us to face loneliness head-on without losing hope.

Self-acceptance, Care and Compassion

Loneliness often stems from feelings of inadequacy or self-judgment. To combat this, it's essential to practice self-acceptance, care, and compassion.

Self-acceptance involves embracing ourselves fully, flaws and all. It means recognizing that we are worthy of love and belonging, regardless of our perceived shortcomings. Through self-care practices such as exercise, healthy eating, and adequate rest, we can nurture our physical and emotional well-being.

Compassion, both for ourselves and others, is also crucial in combating loneliness. By cultivating a compassionate mindset, we can extend kindness and understanding to ourselves, soothing the inner critic that fuels feelings of isolation.

Creating Your New Self-Image and Ideal Self

Loneliness can distort our self-image, leading us to believe that we are unworthy of connection or happiness. To combat this, it's essential to create a new self-image rooted in self-love and authenticity.

Start by envisioning your ideal self – the person you aspire to be. What qualities does this person possess? How do they interact with others? By aligning our actions with this ideal self, you can gradually reshape your self-image and cultivate a greater sense of confidence and self-worth.

Remember, self-image is not fixed – it's something that can evolve and change over time. By practicing self-reflection and self-awareness, you can continually refine your self-image and move closer to your ideal self.

Focus on Results

Ultimately, overcoming loneliness is about taking action and focusing on results. Set tangible goals for yourself – whether it's joining a social club, volunteering, or reaching out to old friends. By taking proactive steps to connect with others and engage in meaningful activities, you can gradually chip away at loneliness and create a more fulfilling life.

But remember, progress takes time, and setbacks are inevitable.

You cannot unthink a thought, but you can create a new and more powerful thought that replaces the old one.

By being patient and by staying focused on your goals and believing in your ability to overcome loneliness, you can create a brighter, more connected future for yourself.

In the following chapters we will delve deeper into different tools, and techniques, provide you with exercises to empower you to break free from the cycle.

Part 5: The Power of Prayer in Combating Loneliness

Loneliness can often feel like a heavy burden, weighing down our spirits and leaving us feeling disconnected from the world around us. In times of isolation and solitude, prayer can serve as a beacon of hope, offering solace, connection, and guidance.

A Source of Comfort and Solace

In moments of loneliness, prayer provides a comforting refuge—a sacred space where we can pour out our hearts and express our deepest emotions. Whether we're grappling with feelings of isolation, longing for companionship, or wrestling with inner turmoil, prayer offers a safe haven where we can seek solace and find peace.

Through prayer, we can connect with a higher power, whether we conceive of it as God, the universe, or our inner wisdom. This connection brings a sense of reassurance, reminding us that we are never truly alone—that there is a divine presence that listens to our prayers and offers comfort in our times of need.

A Pathway to Connection and Community

Loneliness often stems from a sense of disconnectedness—from feeling estranged from others and ourselves. Prayer can help bridge this divide, serving as a pathway to connection and community.

In many religious traditions, prayer is a communal practice—a shared experience that brings people together in worship, fellowship, and mutual support. Whether it's through group prayers at a place of worship or virtual gatherings online, prayer provides an opportunity to connect with like-minded individuals who share our beliefs and values.

Even in moments of solitary prayer, we are never truly alone. Through our prayers, we can feel connected to a larger spiritual community—a community that spans across time and space, transcending the boundaries of individuality and fostering a sense of belonging.

A Source of Guidance and Direction

Loneliness can often leave us feeling adrift, unsure of where to turn or how to navigate the complexities of life. In these moments, prayer can offer guidance and direction, helping us find clarity amidst the confusion and uncertainty.

Through prayer, we can seek wisdom and discernment, asking for guidance in making important decisions or facing difficult challenges.

Whether it's through silent meditation, reciting sacred texts, or engaging in heartfelt conversations with a higher power, prayer can help us tap into a source of inner strength and intuition, guiding us along the path towards greater fulfillment and purpose.

A Practice of Gratitude and Reflection

Loneliness can sometimes overshadow the blessings that surround us, blinding us to the beauty and abundance of life. Prayer offers an antidote to this negativity, inviting us to cultivate an attitude of gratitude and reflection.

Through prayer, we can express gratitude for the blessings we've received—the love of family and friends, the beauty of nature, the gift of life itself. By acknowledging these blessings, we can shift our perspective from one of lack to one of abundance, finding solace in the knowledge that we are richly blessed, even in our moments of solitude.

Prayer also provides an opportunity for self-reflection, allowing us to pause and ponder the deeper questions of existence. Through prayerful introspection, we can gain insight into our own inner workings—our hopes and fears, strengths and weaknesses—leading to greater self-awareness and personal growth.

Finding Connection in the Sacred

In the depths of loneliness, prayer serves as a lifeline—a source of comfort, connection, and guidance in an often turbulent world. Whether we turn to prayer in times of crisis or as a daily practice of spiritual nourishment, its power to combat loneliness is undeniable.

Through prayer, we find solace in the knowledge that we are never truly alone—that a higher power watches over us, guiding us with love and compassion. In the sacred space of prayer, we find connection and community, joining with others in a shared journey of faith and fellowship. And in the quiet moments of reflection and gratitude, we find peace amidst the storms of life, embracing the beauty and abundance that surrounds us.

So let us embrace the power of prayer—not merely as a religious ritual, but as a profound act of communion with the divine, a sacred practice that brings comfort to the soul and light to the darkness of loneliness.

"Self-care is not selfish. You cannot serve from an empty vessel." -
Eleanor Brown

Part 6: Practicing Self-care and nourishment

Self-care is a vital aspect of maintaining our mental, emotional, and physical well-being. In this chapter, we explore how cultivating self-care practices that nurture and rejuvenate us, allows us to thrive in all aspects of our lives.

Self-care involves prioritizing our mental and emotional health by engaging in activities that promote relaxation, stress reduction, and emotional resilience. By incorporating self-care practices into our daily routines, we can enhance our overall well-being and build resilience to life's challenges.

Introduction to Mindfulness, Meditation, and Relaxation Techniques:

Here is an opportunity to explore different mindfulness, meditation, and relaxation techniques and discover which ones resonate most with you. This is not an exhaustive list but reflects some of the most common techniques with no capital cost required to implement them.

Mindfulness, meditation, and relaxation techniques are powerful tools for managing stress, reducing anxiety, and enhancing overall well-being. In this section, you will receive an introduction to these practices and learn how they can benefit your mental and emotional health.

Key concepts covered include:

> *Mindfulness: Being aware and fully present in the moment and being a pure witness to our thoughts, feelings/emotions and actions.*

> *Meditation: Practicing focused attention and concentration to cultivate inner peace and clarity of mind.*

> *Relaxation techniques: Using breathing exercises, progressive muscle relaxation, and guided imagery to induce a state of calm and relaxation.*

Guided Mindfulness Exercise: Practicing Self-Compassion and Relaxation:

In this experiential exercise, you will engage in a guided mindfulness practice focused on cultivating self-compassion and relaxation. This will be led through a series of mindfulness exercises, including:

> **Body scan meditation:** Bringing attention to different parts of the body and noticing sensations without judgment.

> Find a comfortable position, either sitting or lying down, where you can relax without any distractions.

> Close your eyes and take a few deep breaths to help you be fully present with yourself.

Start by bringing your attention to your feet. Notice any sensations you feel there, such as warmth, tingling, or pressure.

Slowly move your attention up through your body, one body part at a time, noticing any sensations you encounter along the way.

Pay attention to your legs, hips, stomach, chest, arms, hands, neck, and head.

If you notice any areas of tension or discomfort, simply acknowledge them without trying to change them. Allow them to be as they are.

Finish the practice by taking a few deep breaths and gently bringing your awareness back to the present moment.

Loving-kindness meditation:
Sending wishes of kindness and compassion to oneself and others.

Find a comfortable and quiet space to sit or lie down.

Close your eyes and take a few deep breaths to relax your body and mind.

Begin by directing loving-kindness towards yourself.

Repeat phrases such as:

"I am happy, I am healthy, I am safe, I am Love, I live with ease. I love myself unconditionally" (add more affirmations and state them as if it has already occurred or what you want as a desired outcome.)Say these phrases with sincerity and compassion.

Next, think of someone you care about deeply, such as a friend or family member. Imagine sending them feelings of love and kindness.

Continue this practice by extending loving-kindness to other people in your life, such as acquaintances, colleagues, and even people you may have conflicts with.

Finally, expand your loving-kindness to include all beings everywhere, repeating the phrases with a sense of universal compassion.

Take a few moments to bask in the feelings of love and kindness that you've cultivated before gently bringing your awareness back to the present moment.

Breath Awareness:

Find a comfortable seated position by sitting upright (in a position that you are comfortable which exerts any pressure on your body to breathe heavily or quicker) and your feet flat on the floor.

Close your eyes

Observing your breath as it enters and leaves the body, anchoring attention in the present moment.

Continue this until you breathe effortlessly, without holding your breath and experience relaxation.

Incorporating Mindfulness, Meditation, and Relaxation Techniques into Daily Life:

Mindfulness, meditation, and relaxation techniques are powerful tools for reducing stress, increasing self-awareness, and promoting inner peace.

Tips:
- Before you step out of bed, spend a few minutes of mindfulness meditation to set a positive tone for the day ahead.
- Practice deep breathing exercises throughout the day to calm your mind and center yourself during moments of stress or anxiety.
- Keeping repeatedly visualizing your ideal self. Imagine how you would act, think and feel. What are the thoughts that excite you about your new self and gradually bring them into everyday activities, such as eating, walking, or washing dishes, by bringing your full attention to the present moment.
- Practice self-compassion and kindness toward yourself, especially during times of stress or difficulty.

- Set aside time each day for activities that bring you joy and relaxation, whether it's reading a book, taking a bath, or listening to music.
- Engage in activities that nourish your soul and replenish your energy, such as spending time in nature, practicing creative expression, or volunteering in your community.

Through this guided exercise, you will experience a sense of calm and relaxation while developing greater self-compassion and acceptance.

Exploring Self-Care Strategies to Boost Mental and Emotional Health:

Self-care is essential for maintaining overall well-being and resilience, especially in times of stress or difficulty. In this section, you will explore various self-care strategies that promote mental and emotional health. These include:

- Engaging in activities that bring joy and fulfillment
- Setting boundaries and practicing assertiveness
- Prioritizing rest and relaxation
- Nurturing social connections
- Seeking professional help when needed

Exercise 6: Creating a Personalized Self-Care Plan:

In this exercise, you will create a personalized self-care plan tailored to your individual needs and preferences. You will reflect on the self-care practices explored in the book and identify specific ways you intend to incorporate them into your daily routine.
Key components of the self-care plan may include:

- Identifying self-care activities that bring joy, relaxation, and fulfillment
- Setting realistic goals for incorporating self-care into daily life
- Establishing a schedule or routine for engaging in self-care practices
- Anticipating potential barriers to self-care and brainstorming ideas for overcoming them

By the end of this book, you will leave with a concrete plan for prioritizing your well-being and incorporating self-care into your daily life. Let's do this!

Engaging in Activities that Bring Joy and Fulfillment:

Self-care isn't just about relaxation and stress reduction; it's also about nurturing our passions, interests, and sense of purpose. By engaging in activities that bring us joy and fulfillment, we can cultivate a greater sense of meaning and satisfaction in our lives.

Tips:
- Make time for hobbies and activities that you enjoy, whether it's painting, gardening, or playing a musical instrument.
- Spend time with loved ones who uplift and inspire you, fostering meaningful connections and shared experiences.
- Set goals and pursue interests that align with your values and aspirations, allowing you to live a more purposeful and fulfilling life.

30-Day Self-Care Challenge:

Embark on a 30-day self-care challenge to prioritize your well-being and cultivate healthy habits. Each day, commit to engaging in a self-care activity or practice that nourishes your mind, body, or spirit. Keep track of your progress and reflect on how these practices impact your overall well-being at the end of the challenge.

- Reach out to at least one friend or family member or acquaintance each day.
- Participate in social activities or events at least once a week.
- Practice self-care activities, such as exercise, meditation, or hobbies, regularly.
- Challenge negative thoughts and beliefs about yourself and your relationships.

- Add your own plans to the list

Cultivating self-care practices is essential for nurturing our mental, emotional, and physical well-being. By incorporating plans for self-care into our daily lives, such as prioritizing activities that bring us joy and fulfillment, practicing mindfulness and relaxation techniques, and engaging in regular self-care activities, we can enhance our overall quality of life and build resilience to life's challenges. In the chapters that follow, we will explore additional ideas for fostering well-being and building a life filled with meaning and purpose.

"Listening is a magnetic and strange thing, a creative force. The friends who listen to us are the ones we move toward. When we are listened to, it creates us, makes us unfold and expand." - Karl A. Menninger

Part 7: Keeping Personal Relationships Alive

Sustaining meaningful relationships over time requires effort, patience, and understanding. In this chapter, we delve into practical tips for maintaining long-term connections, navigating conflicts and challenges in relationships.

Re-igniting long-term personal connections

These connections, often rooted in shared history, mutual understanding, and genuine affection, provide a sense of belonging and support that can alleviate feelings of isolation. By reaching out to old friends, family members, or acquaintances, we can tap into a rich reservoir of meaningful relationships that have the potential to reignite our sense of connection and purpose.

Whether it's through a heartfelt phone call, a handwritten letter, or a spontaneous meet-up, nurturing these long-term connections reminds us that we are not alone in our journey and that there are people who care about us deeply. In rekindling these relationships, we not only combat loneliness but also create opportunities for shared laughter, shared memories, and shared moments of joy, strengthening the bonds that sustain us through life's ups and downs.

Tips for Sustaining Meaningful Relationships Over Time:

Building lasting connections involves nurturing trust, communication, and shared experiences. Here are some practical tips for maintaining long-term connections:

Consistent Communication:

Regularly check in with loved ones through phone calls, text messages, or in-person visits to show that you care and value their presence in your life.

Quality Time Together:

Make time for shared activities and experiences that strengthen your bond, whether it's going for walks, cooking together, or attending events and gatherings.

Express Appreciation:

Show gratitude for the people in your life by expressing appreciation for their support, kindness, and companionship. Small gestures of appreciation can go a long way in sustaining meaningful relationships.

Think of relationships as plants in a garden. Just as plants require regular watering, sunlight, and care to thrive, relationships need consistent nurturing and attention to flourish over time.

Don't make excuses!!

This, in my understanding, is the biggest problem! You love me or hate me. It is true!

Mary and David have been friends since college. Despite living in different cities, they make an effort to stay connected by scheduling regular video calls and planning annual get-togethers. They express gratitude for each other's friendship and make time for shared interests, such as hiking and exploring new restaurants together.

Dealing with Conflicts and Challenges in Relationships:

Conflicts and challenges are inevitable in any relationship, but how we navigate them can determine the strength and resilience of our connections. Here are some ways of addressing conflicts and challenges in relationships:

Open Communication:

Foster open and honest communication by expressing your thoughts and feelings calmly and respectfully. Listening actively to the other person's perspective is important. It doesn't imply that you agree or accept what they have to say. It simply shows that you respect their views. Every person has a right to be heard and understood.

Accommodating and Flexibility:

Be willing to make adjustments and adapt to changing circumstances to find common ground and maintain harmony in your relationships. Flexibility and understanding can help navigate conflicts more effectively.

Outcome over ego:

Often in conflicts it's our ego that tends to influence the choice we make. Letting go of your ego in most situations can prove to be very beneficial by focussing our actions on the outcomes we truly want.

Imagine relationships as ships navigating stormy seas. Just as ships rely on skilled captains and crew members to navigate turbulent waters, relationships require effective communication and cooperation to weather challenges and reach calmer shores.

Maintaining long-term connections requires intentionality, communication, and flexibility. By implementing practical tips for sustaining meaningful relationships, navigating conflicts and challenges, and coping with periods of solitude, we can cultivate deeper connections with others and foster a sense of belonging and fulfillment in our lives.

Living in Solitude:

For those who have lost all family members, finding strength amidst profound grief and solitude can seem like an insurmountable challenge. Yet, within the depths of your sorrow lies a resilience born of unimaginable adversity. In the absence of familial bonds, you can discover an inner fortitude—a wellspring of courage and perseverance that will sustain you through the darkest of days.

Draw strength from cherished memories, knowing that the love shared with your lost loved ones endures in your heart forever. Though the journey may be marked by solitude, you are not alone, for within is the indomitable spirit of your family's legacy—a beacon of hope that guides you through the storm. And in resilience, you find solace, knowing that you have capacity to endure, to heal, and to thrive is a testament to the unbreakable human spirit.

In the chapters that follow, we will explore additional tools for fostering resilience, well-being, and connection in our personal and social lives.

"You yourself, as much as anybody in the entire universe, deserve your love and affection." - Buddha

Part 8: Nurturing Social Connections

Importance of Building and Maintaining Supportive Relationships:

Social connections are essential for our well-being, providing us with support, companionship, and a sense of belonging. In this chapter, we will explore how to build and maintain meaningful relationships, develop effective communication skills, and find communities that resonate with our interests and values.

Building and maintaining supportive relationships is crucial for combating loneliness and fostering a sense of belonging. Strong social connections provide emotional support, companionship, and a sense of belonging, which can help alleviate feelings of isolation and loneliness. By investing time and effort into nurturing these relationships, you can cultivate a support network that enriches your life and enhances your overall well-being.

Building and Maintaining Supportive Friendships and Relationships: Meaningful relationships are built on trust, mutual respect, and shared experiences. By investing time and effort into nurturing these connections, we can cultivate strong bonds that withstand the test of time.

Tips:

- Prioritize quality over quantity when it comes to friendships.
- Make time for regular check-ins and meaningful conversations.
- Show empathy and compassion toward your friends' experiences and emotions.
- Be reliable and supportive during times of need.

Effective Communication Skills for Deepening Connections:

Effective communication is essential for fostering intimacy and understanding in relationships. By practicing active listening, expressing ourselves authentically, and being mindful of nonverbal cues, we can deepen our connections with others and strengthen our bonds.

Tips:

- Practice active listening by giving your full attention to the speaker and validating their feelings.
- Be open and honest in your communication, expressing your thoughts and emotions with clarity and respect.
- Pay attention to nonverbal cues such as body language and tone of voice, which can convey important messages.
- Practice empathy and perspective-taking to better understand others' experiences and viewpoints.

By honing communication skills such as active listening, empathy, and assertiveness, we can better understand others, express yourself authentically, and navigate interpersonal dynamics with confidence and clarity. These skills play a key role in building trust, resolving conflicts, and strengthening bonds with others.

Exercise 7:

Below are 20 true or false questions to aid with understanding of effective communication techniques:

1. Active listening involves fully concentrating on what the other person is saying without interrupting.

2. Empathy involves understanding and sharing the feelings of another person.

3. Welcoming constructive criticism is an opportunity for growth and improvement in your communication skills.

4. Asking open-ended questions encourages the other person to provide detailed responses.

5. Non-verbal communication, such as body language and facial expressions, does not play a significant role in effective communication.

6. Assertive communication involves expressing one's thoughts, feelings and needs respectfully and confidently.

7. Mirroring involves mimicking the other person's body language to build rapport and connection.

8. Reflective listening involves reflecting the other person's emotions to show understanding and validation.

9. Validation involves dismissing or minimizing the other person's feelings.

10. Feedback should be specific, constructive, and focused on behavior rather than personality.

11. Giving advice without being asked is an effective way to support someone in distress.

12. Using "I" statements can help express thoughts and feelings assertively without blaming or accusing others.

13. Tone of voice and intonation can significantly impact the interpretation of a message.

14. Providing empathy involves trying to fix the other person's problems or offer solutions.

15. Non-verbal cues, such as eye contact and nodding, can signal attentiveness and understanding during a conversation.

16. Active listening involves mentally preparing responses while the other person is speaking.

17. Reflective listening involves summarizing the other person's message to check for understanding.

18. Empathetic responses should focus on minimizing or dismissing the other person's emotions.

19. Using humor to lighten the mood can be an effective communication strategy in certain situations.

20. Effective communication involves both speaking and listening actively and empathetically.

These quiz questions will aid your knowledge of effective communication techniques and provide an opportunity for reflection on how to enhance communication skills to deepen connections and foster meaningful relationships.

Answer key:

1. True 2. True 3. True 4. True 5. False 6. True 7. True 8. True 9. False 10. True 11. False 12. True 13. True 14. False 15. True 16. False 17. True 18. False 19. True 20. True

Nurturing social connections is essential for our emotional well-being and overall quality of life. By building and maintaining supportive friendships, developing effective communication skills, and finding communities that resonate with our interests and values, we can cultivate deeper connections with others and create a sense of belonging in our lives. In the chapters that follow, we will explore additional strategies for fostering social connections and building a supportive network of relationships.

Just because something doesn't do what you planned it to do doesn't mean it's useless. - *Thomas Edison (Inventor)*

Part 9: Embracing Technology Mindfully

In today's digital age, technology has revolutionized the way we communicate and connect with others. While it offers unprecedented opportunities for connection and community, it can also pose challenges to our well-being if used mindlessly. In this chapter, we explore how to embrace technology mindfully, using it as a tool to enhance our relationships and prioritize real-life connections.

Tool for Connection Rather Than a Barrier:
Technology has the power to bridge geographical distances and connect us with loved ones across the globe. By harnessing the potential of technology mindfully, we can strengthen our relationships, foster meaningful connections, and cultivate a sense of belonging in our digital communities.

Tips:
- Use video calls, messaging apps, and social media platforms to stay connected with friends and family, especially those who live far away. Remember to stay safe online and ensure your safety.
- Share meaningful moments, photos, and updates with loved ones to maintain a sense of closeness and connection.

- Participate in online forums, virtual events, and social media groups related to your interests to connect with like-minded individuals and expand your social network.

Balancing Online Interactions with Face-to-Face Communication: While technology enables us to connect with others virtually, it's essential to balance online interactions with face-to-face communication. Building and maintaining real-life connections through in-person interactions can deepen our relationships and foster a sense of intimacy and connection that cannot be replicated online.

Tips:

- Make time for face-to-face interactions with friends, family, and loved ones whenever possible.
- Plan outings, gatherings, or activities that allow for meaningful, in-person connections.
- Prioritize quality time with loved ones, putting away electronic devices and focusing on being present in the moment.

Setting Boundaries and Managing Screen Time:

In a world where technology is ubiquitous, setting boundaries and managing screen time is crucial for maintaining a healthy balance between online and offline life. By establishing clear boundaries around technology use and prioritizing real-life connections, we can cultivate a more fulfilling and meaningful existence.

Tips:

- Use apps or features that track and limit your screen time to prevent excessive use of electronic devices.
- Prioritize activities that promote well-being and connection, such as exercise, hobbies, and spending time outdoors, over passive screen time.
- Turn off notifications and news feeds
- You set the rules that work

Embracing technology mindfully allows us to harness its potential for connection while preserving the richness and depth of real-life interactions. By using technology as a tool to enhance our relationships, balancing online interactions with face-to-face communication, and setting boundaries to prioritize real-life connections, we can cultivate deeper connections with others and lead more fulfilling lives both online and offline. In the chapters that follow, we will explore additional ways to foster meaningful connections and build a supportive network of relationships.

"Alone we can do so little; together we can do so much." - Helen Keller

Part 10: Embracing Community and Support

A supportive community plays a crucial role in fostering a sense of belonging, connection, and well-being for individuals. In this chapter, we explore the importance of participating in inclusive and supportive environments, fostering a sense of belonging in local communities, workplaces, and online spaces, and promoting empathy, compassion, and understanding in interpersonal relationships.

The Importance of Participating in Inclusive and Supportive Environments:

Inclusive and supportive environments provide you with a sense of safety, acceptance, and belonging, regardless of your background, identity, or experiences. By prioritizing diversity, equity, and inclusion, communities create spaces where everyone feels valued, respected, and empowered to thrive.

Volunteering: A Catalyst for Connection

Loneliness often feels like a solitary journey, but it's in giving to others that we discover the profound power of human connection. Volunteering isn't just about lending a helping hand; it's about forging meaningful relationships, finding purpose, and breaking free from the cycle of isolation.

Discovering Purpose Through Service

When we volunteer our time and talents to support others, we discover a sense of purpose that transcends our own needs and desires. Whether it's serving meals at a local shelter, tutoring children, or caring for animals at a rescue center, each act of service reminds us that we are part of something greater than ourselves. By contributing to the well-being of others, we find fulfillment and meaning in our lives, enriching our sense of self-worth and purpose.

Forging Genuine Connections

Volunteering brings people together from diverse backgrounds and walks of life, creating opportunities for genuine connection and camaraderie. Whether you're working side by side with fellow volunteers or interacting with those you serve, volunteering fosters a sense of belonging and community that transcends social barriers. Through shared experiences and common goals, volunteers form bonds that can alleviate feelings of loneliness and isolation, providing a supportive network of like-minded individuals who share a commitment to making a difference in the world.

Empowering Others and Yourself

In giving to others, we empower not only those we serve but also ourselves. Volunteering allows us to use our skills and talents to make a positive impact in the lives of others, fostering a sense of pride and accomplishment. By empowering others to overcome challenges and achieve their goals, we experience the joy of making a difference, boosting our self-esteem and confidence in the process. As we witness the transformative power of our actions, we gain a deeper appreciation for our own resilience and potential, breaking free from the limitations imposed by loneliness and self-doubt.

Building Social Skills and Resilience

For many individuals struggling with loneliness, social interactions can be daunting and intimidating. Volunteering provides a safe and supportive environment to practice and improve social skills, allowing volunteers to build confidence and resilience in their interactions with others. Whether it's initiating conversations, working as part of a team, or navigating interpersonal dynamics, volunteering offers valuable opportunities for personal growth and development. As volunteers step outside of their comfort zones and engage with others in meaningful ways, they gain the skills and confidence needed to overcome social barriers and cultivate deeper connections in their personal lives.

Embracing Connection Through Service

Volunteering is more than just a charitable act; it's a powerful tool for combating loneliness and fostering connection in our communities. By discovering purpose through service, forging genuine connections, empowering others and ourselves, and building social skills and resilience, volunteers can break free from the cycle of isolation and embrace a life filled with meaning, fulfillment, and belonging. So, let's roll up our sleeves, lend a helping hand, and together, let's weave a tapestry of connection and compassion that binds us all.

Sense of Belonging:
Fostering a sense of belonging requires intentional effort and commitment from individuals and communities alike. You must be willing to take the first step to create opportunities for meaningful connections, promoting collaboration and cooperation, and celebrating diversity and individuality.

Promoting Empathy, Compassion, and Understanding:
Empathy, compassion, and understanding are essential qualities for building supportive relationships and communities. By cultivating empathy for others' experiences, practicing compassion in our interactions, and seeking to understand different perspectives, we can create a more inclusive and harmonious society.

John, a 45-year-old man, lived alone in a small apartment in the heart of the city. Despite being surrounded by bustling streets and crowded sidewalks, John felt profoundly isolated from the world around him.

Working long hours at a demanding job, John had little time for socializing, and his few attempts to connect with coworkers or neighbors fell flat. As a result, he found himself spending most evenings and weekends alone, with only his thoughts for company.

Though he tried to fill the void with hobbies and distractions, the loneliness weighed heavily on John's spirit. He longed for meaningful connections with others, but the geographical distance, physical barriers, and lack of social support networks made it difficult for him to reach out.

It wasn't until John reached out to a local community center for support that he began to see a glimmer of hope. Through the center's programs and events, he was able to meet new people and forge friendships that lifted his spirits and brightened his days.

With the support of his newfound community, John was able to overcome his social isolation and rediscover the joy of human connection. Today, he remains an active member of his community, grateful for the bonds he has formed and the sense of belonging he has found.

Finding Communities and Groups with Common Interests and Values:

Finding like-minded individuals who share our interests and values can provide a sense of belonging and camaraderie. Whether through hobbies, clubs, or online communities, connecting with others who share our passions can enrich our lives and expand our social network.

Tips:

- Explore local meetups, clubs, or interest groups related to your hobbies or interests.
- Join online forums, social media groups, or virtual communities focused on topics you're passionate about.
- Attend events, workshops, or conferences where you can connect with others who share your values and aspirations.
- Be proactive in reaching out and initiating conversations with potential new friends or acquaintances.

In the event you are unable to find a group in your local area we encourage you to take the lead and consider starting one. All you need is just another person to join and get started.

Starting a group to Foster a Sense of Belonging in Local Communities and Online Spaces:

Fostering a sense of belonging in local communities and online spaces is crucial for building strong connections and supportive networks.

These may include:

- Hosting inclusive events and activities that bring people together

- Creating online forums or social media groups for sharing interests and experiences

- Providing opportunities for meaningful participation and contribution

- Offering support and resources for individuals experiencing social isolation or loneliness

Exercise 8: Planning a Community Connection Event:

Use this opportunity to put your ideas into action by planning a community connection event. Here are some suggestions to develop a detailed plan for an event that fosters a sense of belonging and brings people together. Key elements of the event planning exercise may include:

- Setting clear objectives and goals for the event
- Identifying target audience and stakeholders
- Choosing a date, location, and format for the event
- Developing a program agenda and activities
- Creating a promotional plan to attract participants
-Establishing roles and responsibilities for event coordination and execution

By engaging in this section, you will learn how to create inclusive and supportive environments, foster a sense of belonging, and actively contribute to community-building initiatives both offline and online.

"The only way to make sense out of change is to plunge into it, move with it, and join the dance." - Alan Watts

Part 11: Taking Action and Moving Forward

Taking action is the key to overcoming loneliness and building meaningful connections in our lives. In this chapter, we'll guide you through creating a personalized action plan, setting realistic goals, tracking progress, and staying motivated on your journey towards connection and fulfillment.

Creating a Personalized Action Plan:

To combat loneliness effectively, it's essential to create a personalized action plan tailored to your unique needs and circumstances. Here's how to get started:

1. **Self-Reflection:** Take some time to reflect on your current feelings of loneliness and identify specific areas where you'd like to see improvement.

2. **Identify Resources:** Consider the resources and support systems available to you, such as friends, family, community organizations, and mental health professionals.

3. **Set Goals:** Establish realistic and achievable goals for yourself, focusing on areas such as expanding your social network, improving communication skills, and prioritizing self-care.

Exercise 9:

Self-Care Plan Checklist

1. Identify Your Needs:

- Reflect on your physical, emotional, and mental well-being.
- Identify areas where you may need more support or self-care.

2. Set Realistic Goals:

- Define specific, achievable goals for your self-care plan.
- Break down large goals into smaller, manageable steps.

3. Prioritize Self-Care Activities:

- Make a list of self-care activities that resonate with you.
- Prioritize activities that bring you joy, relaxation and fulfillment.

4. Establish a Routine:

- Create a schedule or routine for engaging in self-care practices.

5. Practice Mindfulness:

- Incorporate mindfulness techniques into your daily routine.
- Practice mindfulness meditation, deep breathing exercises, or mindful journaling.

- Use the power of prayer to help you with mindfulness

6. Nurture Social Connections:
- Make time for meaningful interactions with friends and loved ones.
- Reach out to others for support and companionship when needed.

7. Engage in Physical Activity:
- Include regular exercise or physical activity in your self-care plan.
- Choose activities that you enjoy and that align with your ability and goals.

8. Eat Well and Stay Hydrated:
- Pay attention to your nutritional needs and nourish your body with healthy foods.
- Drink plenty of water throughout the day to stay hydrated.

9. Get Adequate Rest:
- Prioritize sleep and establish a regular sleep schedule.
- Create a relaxing bedtime routine to promote restful sleep.

10. Practice Relaxation Techniques:

- Incorporate relaxation techniques into your daily routine, such as deep breathing, progressive muscle relaxation, or guided imagery.
- Set aside time for activities that help you unwind and de-stress, such as reading, listening to music, or taking a bath.

11. Limit Screen Time:

- Set boundaries around screen time and digital devices.
- Take regular breaks from screens and engage in offline activities.

12. Set Boundaries:

- Establish boundaries in your relationships and commitments.
- Learn to say no to requests or obligations that drain your energy or overwhelm you.

13. Practice Self-Compassion:

- Be kind and compassionate to yourself, especially during challenging times.
- Practice self-acceptance and forgiveness, and treat yourself with the same kindness you would offer to a friend.

14. Seek Professional Help When Needed:

- Reach out to a therapist or counselor if you're struggling with your mental health.
- Don't hesitate to seek support and guidance from a mental health professional when needed.

15. Evaluate and Adjust:

- Regularly evaluate your self-care plan and make adjustments as needed.
- Be flexible and open to trying new strategies that better meet your needs.

By using this checklist, you can create a personalized self-care plan that supports your overall well-being and helps you prioritize your health and happiness. This plan is a guide to help you design what is best suited to your individual needs. Getting started and taking action is the key.

Exercise 10: Sample Goal cards

Use this template to set your goals, track your progress and celebrate the success after achieving the goals. Plan your goal to break free from loneliness by the end of this week *(post-completion of this book)*, fortnight, end of the month.

Goal: ______________________________

Action Steps:

   1. _________________________________

   2. _________________________________

   3. _________________________________

Completion: ________end of the week/fortnight/end of the month____________

Progress Tracker:

Week 1: ____

Week 2: ____

Week   3:   ____

 Week 4: ____

Celebrate Successes:

  - ____

  - ____

Part 12: Seeking Professional Support

While self-care practices can be powerful tools for managing loneliness, there are times when seeking professional support is necessary to address underlying issues and develop coping strategies. In this chapter, we explore when to consider therapy or counseling for loneliness, different therapeutic approaches for addressing loneliness and related mental health issues, and resources for finding affordable or free mental health support.

When to Consider Therapy or Counseling for Loneliness:

Loneliness can have profound effects on our mental and emotional well-being, impacting our quality of life and overall health. If feelings of loneliness persist despite efforts to address them through self-care practices and social connections, it may be beneficial to seek professional support. Therapy or counseling or coaching can provide a safe and supportive space to explore the root causes of loneliness and cultivate healthier patterns of thinking and behavior.

Mark, a 35-year-old marketing executive, has been struggling with feelings of loneliness and isolation since his divorce a year ago. Despite efforts to stay connected with friends and family, Mark finds himself withdrawing from social interactions and experiencing overwhelming sadness and despair. After consulting with his primary care physician, Mark decides to seek therapy to address his feelings of loneliness and develop strategies for rebuilding his social support network.

Different Therapeutic Approaches for Addressing Loneliness:
Therapists and counselors employ various therapeutic approaches to address loneliness and related mental health issues. These may include cognitive-behavioral therapy (CBT), which focuses on identifying and challenging negative thought patterns and behaviors; interpersonal therapy (IPT), which explores interpersonal relationships and communication patterns; and mindfulness-based approaches, which emphasize present-moment awareness and self-compassion.

Emily, a 28-year-old graduate student, struggles with social anxiety and finds it challenging to connect with others. She decides to seek therapy with a certified therapist who specializes in mindfulness-based approaches. Through mindfulness meditation and compassionate self-inquiry, Emily learns to cultivate greater self-awareness and acceptance of her feelings of loneliness, ultimately developing more authentic and fulfilling connections with others.

Resources for Finding Affordable or Free Mental Health Support:
Finding affordable or free mental health support can be challenging, especially for those facing financial constraints. However, there are resources available to help individuals access the care they need.

These may include community mental health centers, university counseling centers, online therapy platforms offering sliding-scale fees, and nonprofit organizations that provide free or low-cost counseling services.

> *Sam, a 45-year-old single parent, is struggling to cope with feelings of loneliness and depression. With limited financial resources, Sam is unsure how to access mental health support. After researching online, Sam discovers a local community mental health center that offers sliding-scale fees based on income. With the support of a therapist at the center, Sam begins to explore the underlying causes of loneliness and develop strategies for building social connections and improving mental well-being.*

Seeking professional support for loneliness can be a crucial step toward healing and growth. Whether through therapy, counseling, or other mental health services, you can find the support and guidance needed to address loneliness and related mental health issues, cultivate healthier patterns of thinking and behavior, and build fulfilling connections with others.

In the case studies presented, working with a qualified therapist has proven beneficial in helping individuals navigate feelings of loneliness and develop strategies for improving their overall well-being.

Tip: Please don't ignore the need to seek help. It's never too late.

Conclusion: Moving Forward with Purpose and Resilience

As we come to the end of this journey together, it's important to reflect on the valuable insights, tips, tools and techniques we've explored to combat loneliness. Throughout this book, we've delved into the depths of understanding loneliness, the power of prayer, discovering ways and approaches for nurturing meaningful connections, practicing self-care, and embracing community support.

Now, as you prepare to embark on the next chapter of your life, I encourage you to carry these learnings with you and continue prioritizing your prayer, self-acceptance, social connections and well-being. Remember, each small step you take towards fostering genuine connections and practicing self-compassion is a powerful act of self-love and resilience.

Take a moment to envision the kind of life you want to create for yourself—one filled with deep purpose, meaningful relationships, moments of joy and fulfillment, and a strong sense of belonging. And know that you have the strength and resources within you to make that vision a reality.

As you move forward, I invite you to **set personal goals** and commitments to combat loneliness in your life. Whether it's

reaching out to a friend you haven't spoken to in a while, **joining a new community group**, or dedicating time each day to **self-care practices**, every action you take brings you one step closer to a life of connection and fulfillment.

Lastly, I encourage you to share the insights and wisdom you've gained from this book with others who may be struggling with loneliness. By recommending this book or sharing your experiences with friends, family, or colleagues, you have the opportunity to make a positive impact in their lives and contribute to building a more connected and compassionate community.

As you close your workbook and step out into the world, remember that you are not alone on this journey. Together, we can overcome loneliness, cultivate meaningful connections, and thrive in a world filled with love and belonging.